My First MANDALAS
Coloring Book

Anna Pomaska

DOVER PUBLICATIONS, INC.
Mineola, New York

Note

Mandala is a word that comes from Sanskrit, a very old language. It means circle. Mandalas are one of the oldest art forms. Rock carvings found all over the world echo their circular form and overlapping shapes. Long ago, mandalas were used to help heal people and as offerings to others. Today they are made just for fun!

Inside there are 30 mandalas for you to color. There are stars, snowflakes, diamonds, and dolphins to name just a few. Use colors that you find in the world around you. Color a fish orange, a flower red, and a cat black. Or use only warm colors, such as yellow, orange, and red. These are the colors of sun and fire. Green, purple, and blue are cool colors. Think of lakes and midnight skies. Grays and browns are called neutral colors. They are dull. Use them alone for an interesting effect or to separate stronger colors. Use all your colors any way you wish. The mandala you create will be unlike any other.

Now get ready to make your own mandala. All you need to start are colored markers, crayons, or colored pencils.

Copyright

Copyright © 2008 by Dover Publications, Inc.
All rights reserved.

Bibliographical Note

My First Mandalas Coloring Book is a new work, first published by Dover Publications, Inc., in 2008.

International Standard Book Number
ISBN-13: 978-0-486-46556-2
ISBN-10: 0-486-46556-X

Manufactured in the United States by RR Donnelley
46556X08   2015
www.doverpublications.com

3 hearts

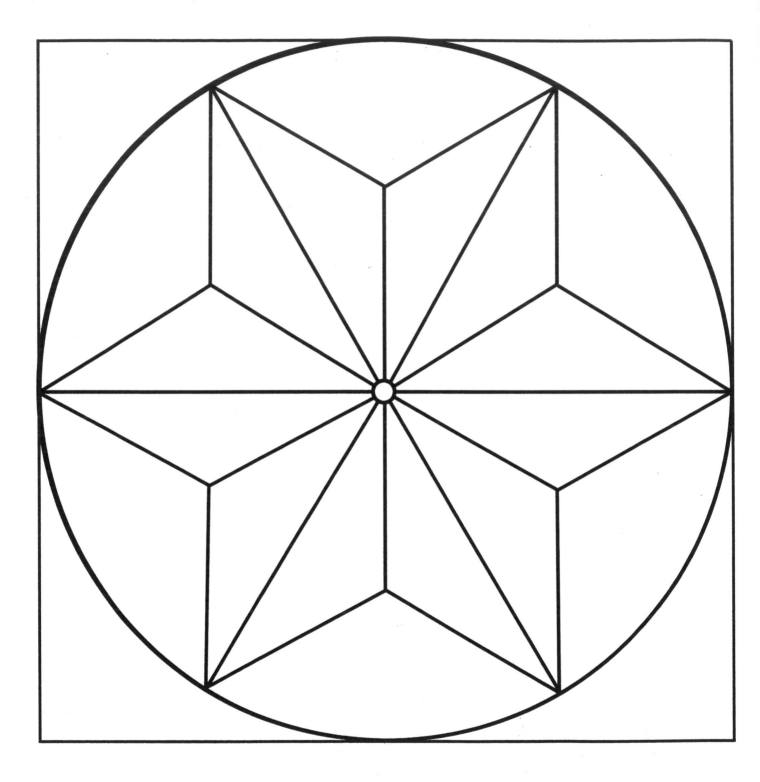

6-point star

Abstract design

Birds

Boats

Butterflies

Cats

Celtic star pattern

Circles

Cross

Diamonds

Dolphins

Elephants

Fish

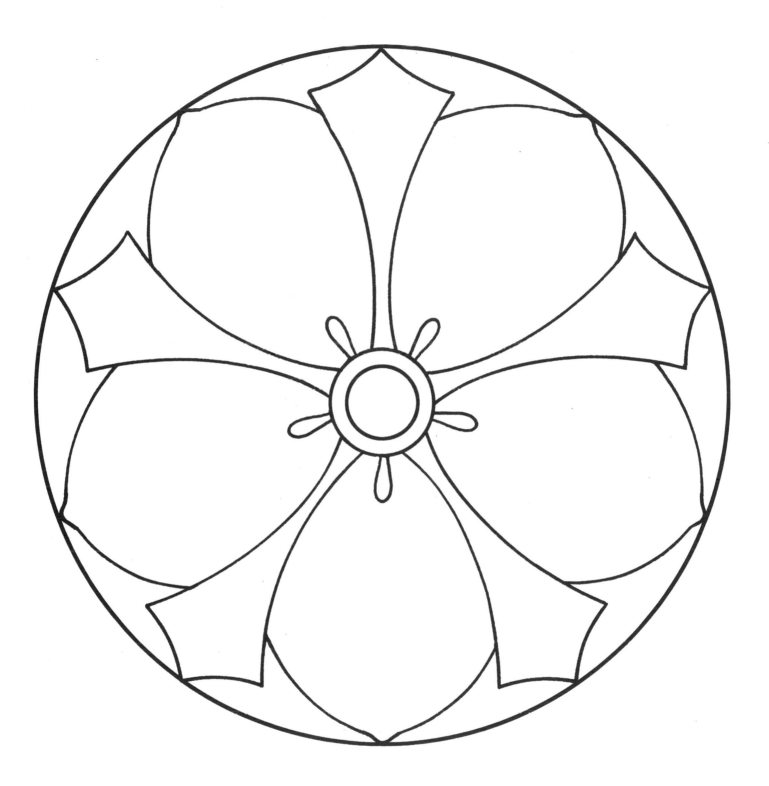

Flower

Frogs

Hands

Heart

Native American design

Kids

Leaves and bugs

Lizards

Moon and sun

Rabbits

Snowflake

Star

Sun and stars

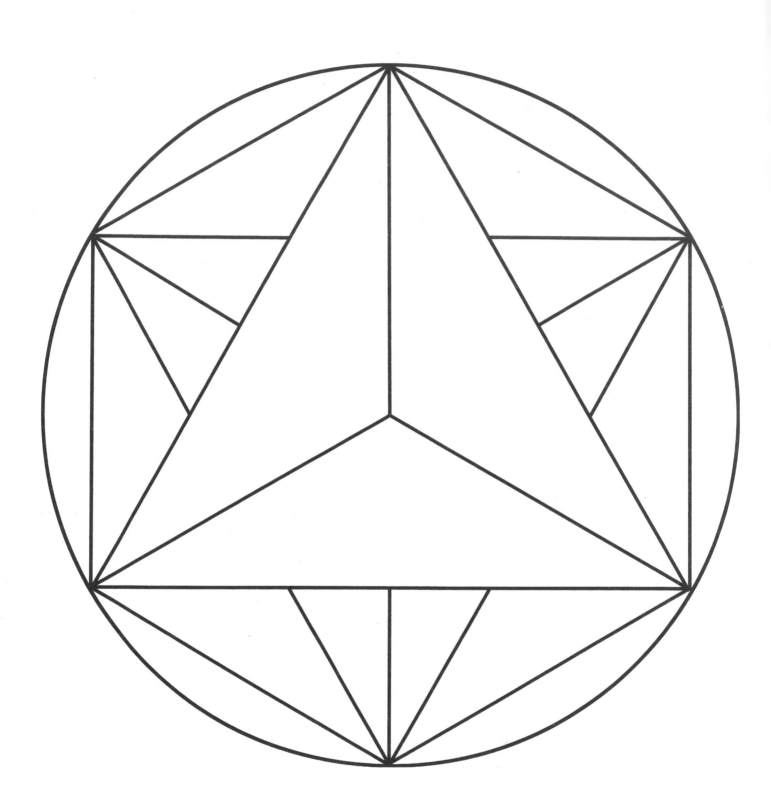

Triangles

Unicorns

Geometric design